HUNTING

FOR FUN!

By Jef Wilson

Content Adviser: Chuck Buzzy, President of Kamp for Kids, Brighton, Michigan
Reading Adviser: Susan Kesselring, M.A., Literacy Educator, Apple Valley, Minnesota

COMPASS POINT BOOKS

MINNEAPOLIS, MINNESOTA

Compass Point Books
3109 West 50th Street, #115
Minneapolis, MN 55410

Visit Compass Point Books on the Internet at www.compasspointbooks.com
or e-mail your request to custserv@compasspointbooks.com

Editors: Deb Berry and Aubrey Whitten/Bill SMITH STUDIO; and Shelly Lyons
Designer/Page Production: Geron Hoy, Kavita Ramchandran, Sinae Sohn, Marina Terletsky, and Brock Waldron/Bill SMITH STUDIO
Photo Researcher: Jacqueline Lissy Brustein, Scott Rosen, and Allison Smith/Bill SMITH STUDIO
Art Director: Jaime Martens
Creative Director: Keith Griffin
Editorial Director: Carol Jones
Managing Editor: Catherine Neitge

Library of Congress Cataloging-in-Publication Data
Wilson, Jef, 1973-
 Hunting for fun! / by Jef Wilson.
   p. cm. -- (For fun!)
 Includes bibliographical references and index.
 ISBN 0-7565-1680-3 (hard cover)
 1. Hunting--Juvenile literature. I. Title. II. Series.
 SK35.5.W55 2005
 799.2--dc22
                          2005025221

Printed in the United States of America.

Table of Contents

The Basics

Doing It

People, Places, and Fun

● ●

Note: In this book, there are two kinds of vocabulary words. Hunting Words to Know are words specific to hunting. They are defined on page 46. Other Words to Know are helpful words that aren't related only to hunting. They are defined on page 47.

The First Sport

Today, we don't think of hunting as a means of survival. But before there were supermarkets and department stores to buy food, clothing, and supplies, people had to hunt to live. In times past, hunting was more than a sport. Hunters today carry on in the tradition of their ancestors.

Although hunting may not be necessary for survival, for avid hunters it is a way of life. Hunters have great respect for nature and wildlife. For many people, part of the thrill of the hunt is "getting back to nature." When you hunt, you have to rely on your own instincts and skills to be successful in the wild.

In the Beginning

Hunting dates back thousands of years, to the beginnings of humankind. Weapons were the first real form of technology. The first tools and weapons, dating back 40,000 years, were created during the Stone Age to help in the hunt.

The earliest known cave art shows hunters chasing bull-like creatures. Animals provided important protein in the diet of ancient people. Before our ancestors learned to plant and farm, hunting and gathering were the methods used to obtain food. Even today, entire villages in Africa depend on hunting for a big part of their food supply.

Hunters also used animal hides (skin or fur) for clothing, including gloves and footwear. Hides and furs were especially important to people in cold climates.

Long ago, the Inuit people in the Arctic made complicated parkas from animal skins. They sewed the skins together and had up to 60 stitched pieces. Parkas kept the Inuit warm, even in temperatures below zero.

The horns and bones of animals were used for making tools, weapons, and ornaments. Hunters wasted very little.

A 40,000-year-old cave painting of a man hunting

Keeping Nature Balanced

In nature, wildlife and plants coexist in a delicate balance called an ecosystem. An ecosystem is a community of plants, animals, and everything in their environment. The plants and animals in an ecosystem need to have the right balance with each other and with their environment to survive.

In each state, conservation departments study ecosystems. In the United States, there are many types of land areas, from deserts to mountains. This is why the United States is home to so many different types of wildlife, especially in the forests.

Too few of any species of animal can create an imbalance in the ecosystem. It can even lead to extinction of a species. But what many people don't realize is that too many of a certain animal can also ruin a natural environment. This is called overpopulation, and it can be dangerous for people and other animals. Overpopulation of any living species can cause great damage to natural habitats.

North American elk

11

Gearing Up

As a hunter, you will need a lot of the same equipment that hikers and campers use. Durable clothing and good hiking boots, made of leather and rubber, are essential. Because people hunt in all kids of weather, cold weather gear with several layers of insulation, or a material that holds in heat, may be necessary. Sleeping bags and tents are needed for hunting trips that last more than a day.

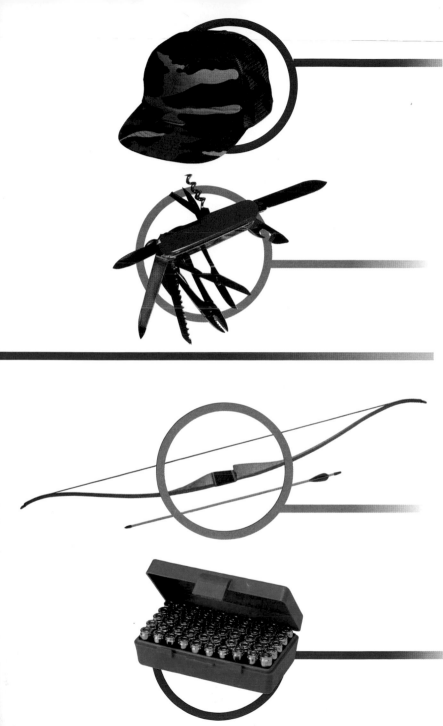

Many hunters wear camouflage clothing. This helps them avoid being seen by the animals they hunt.

You'll need a backpack to carry food, water, and other equipment such as maps, a compass, sunglasses, a pocketknife, and a flashlight.

You should wear bright colored orange clothes, because most animals can only see in black and white. However, you must make yourself visible to other hunters.

You'll need your weapon of choice, like a bow and arrows, depending on what type of game you'll be hunting.

If you plan to use a firearm, you will need to bring ammunition such as bullets, shot, or BBs.

On Your Mark

Hunters often learn skills from family members who pass knowledge from generation to generation. Another way to learn about hunting is to take classes and seminars. Taking classes is a good idea, even for experienced hunters. State conservation departments usually offer hunting instruction.

Important classes include gun safety and proper use of firearms, archery, regional wildlife study and tracking, outdoor survival, and hunting rules and etiquette, or manners. Check with your local conservation department for information about classes.

Basic target shooting and archery are fun ways to start practicing the skills you need to become a good hunter. The more you practice, the better and more accurate your aim will become.

Safety First

Any time you handle or use weapons, you should be supervised by an experienced adult.

The Law of the Land

To be able to hunt at all, you must have a hunting permit. Nearly all types of hunting have a season (length of time) when it is legal to hunt certain animals. Every state has its own laws and regulations.

In most states, large game is closely watched by authorities. Usually within the season, there are strict limits on the number of animals you can take. Hunters are required to buy a tag for each animal they wish to hunt. This means, if you hunt animals like deer, elk, or bear, you must buy a tag for each animal in addition to a hunting permit. Most tags are bought in the fall during deer season. Special licenses or tags are also required to hunt waterfowl, like ducks and geese, and upland fowl, like quail, pheasant, and wild turkey.

The only federal hunting laws are those that regulate hunting of migratory birds, or birds that move from one climate to another.

Get a License!

Hunting without a license can result in serious penalties and fines, so make sure you always check the hunting laws of your state before you start.

Knowing Your Sport

It takes skill, knowledge, and patience to become a good hunter. Good hunters are knowledgeable about wildlife, their habits, and nature. They are good at tracking and identifying animals. It takes different sets of skills to hunt turkeys, waterfowl, and small and big game. Also, each requires a different type of firearm and ammunition.

To be a good hunter, you must always handle your weapons in a safe way and practice using them. Being able to "sight in" a firearm is important. This means adjusting the sights on a gun to match where the shot actually goes. Other important skills include judging distance, field dressing (preparing a recently killed animal so that its body temperature lowers and the meat remains fresh), knowing when (and when not) to shoot, hunting ethics (accepted behaviors), conservation, and overall safety. Education is the key to becoming an ethical, skillful, and successful hunter.

Start Out Small

After completing hunting and safety classes and practicing your aim, you are ready to start hunting. Hunting small game, such as squirrels and rabbits, is a great way to begin. Because these animals are small and quick on their feet, the hunt can be very challenging.

For hunting small game, there are a few options for weaponry. A basic bow and arrow is one option.

Another is an air gun. "Ammo" (short for ammunition) for air guns includes BBs and pellets. BBs are small, round, and made of metal. Pellets are also made of metal, but are blunt at the front, and flare out a little at the back.

A third option is a small caliber firearm, like a .22 caliber rifle. The .22 caliber bullet is a little larger than a BB and goes much farther when fired.

Gobble, Gobble!

Because turkeys see so well, their hunters often wear camouflage face paint. Some say that, even from far away, turkeys can see the whites of your eyes!

Most rabbits are hunted for both their meat and fur.

Archery in Hunting

Archery is the sport of shooting arrows with a bow. The bow and arrow is a very popular weapon choice for many hunters.

Choosing the right bow depends on the hunter's size and strength. Bows are rated in pounds. If a bow is rated 70 pounds, it will take 70 pounds (32 kg) of strength to pull back the string that shoots the arrow. The harder it is to pull the string, the farther the arrow will go.

It is important to get a bow that matches your strength and skill. Various types of arrows and arrowheads are also available, depending on the type of game they are used to shoot.

The Atlatl

The atlatl is believed to have been the first hunting weapon. It has been used since the Upper Paleolithic era, 18,000 to 16,000 B.C. It was a large wooden dart–up to 6 feet (1.8 meters) long–that could be thrown up to 50 feet (15.3 meters)!

Rifles and Shotguns

The two basic types of hunting firearms are rifles and shotguns. Each rifle is made to shoot a certain size of bullet or ammunition. There are different sizes of ammunition used for different types of game.

Shotguns shoot bullets that are made of many small pieces called "shot," instead of just one bullet. When the gun is fired, the shot spreads out and covers a larger area. Like the rifle ammunition, shot comes in different sizes, for different uses. For example, birdshot contains many small pieces about half the size and shape of a BB. Buckshot contains fewer, larger pieces about twice the size and shape of a BB. As you might guess, birdshot is used to shoot birds, and buckshot is used to shoot bucks, or male deer.

The standard rifle doesn't weigh much. The weight can range between 7 pounds (3 kg) and 7½ pounds (3.5 kg). If you add a scope the weight increases about a pound.

Scope This Out

A scope is like a miniature telescope mounted on the top of a rifle. A standard scope uses 5x magnification. This means when you look through it you will see your target five times the size you would normally see it. The scope helps you aim, when you line up its guides with your target.

Tree Stands and Ground Blinds

Once you have the hang of basic hunting skills, advanced hunting equipment can make your hunt more successful. Tree stands are used by hunters to hunt from trees. They allow hunters to stalk prey up high so the animals cannot see them. A good tree stand is lightweight and easy to set up and take down.

Ground blinds are very popular with bow hunters. Blinds are used in the same way as tree stands. They allow hunters to stay in one place, where animals cannot see them. Unlike tree stands, blinds are set up on the ground and blend in more with the surroundings. Most serious bow hunters have a good quality blind for times when tree stands are not an option. If you plan to hunt turkeys, a good blind will be very helpful.

A Hunter's Best Friend

There's a saying that "dog is man's best friend." This may be most true for the hunter. Many hunters rely on special dogs that are trained to assist them in the hunt. Hunting dogs use their senses of sight, sound, and smell to track all kinds of animals. Because of their keener senses, they are able to track and locate animals in ways that a human hunter cannot.

"Gun dogs" (often retrievers) help hunters who use firearms. These dogs are trained not to fear the sound of guns firing. They will usually locate the prey and point out their location to the hunter.

"Bird dogs" (usually setters, pointers, or spaniels) are trained to freeze when they have spotted birds in hiding. Whatever your prey as a hunter, you can most likely find a dog that will help you.

Even small breeds such as dachshunds and terriers can help a hunter track small game.

Golden Retriever

Spaniel

Bloodhound

Do the Right Thing

It is important to hunt by the rules, with both the proper training and permits. This is part of being an ethical hunter. When people break the rules, it can lead to lands becoming restricted or banned from public use.

One big problem is poaching, or illegal hunting. Poaching includes hunting animals that are out of season or protected by laws like the Endangered Species Act. Poaching causes many problems for the environment and for hunters who obey the laws.

It is also illegal to trespass or enter a person's private property. Hunting animals on someone's private land without permission is considered a form of poaching, even if the animal is in season.

Park rangers or forest rangers are law enforcement officers who protect and preserve parklands and forests. They enforce the rules, often in remote wilderness areas. Rules regarding poaching and trespassing are strictly enforced. There can be harsh penalties for not following the rules.

The Endangered Species Act

In 1973 laws were passed that protected many species of animals whose numbers were so small that they were at risk of extinction. The ivory-billed woodpecker and Arakan forest turtle are two examples of animals that are at high risk of extinction.

Endangered North American mountain lion

Archery and Shooting

Two of the main skills used in hunting, archery and shooting, are competitive events in the Olympics.

The Olympic archery competition was part of the original Olympic games, when they began nearly 3,000 years ago in ancient Greece. It takes place outdoors, in four categories: Individual men's and women's, and men's and women's team events. Competitors shoot at a target of 10 colored concentric, or layered, circles known as rings. An arrow in the center circle (known as the bull's eye) is worth 10 points, while an arrow in the outer circle is worth one. An arrow landing in a ring between the bull's eye and outer circle is worth anywhere from two to nine points, depending on how close it is to the center.

The shooting competitions are more complicated. There are 17 Olympic shooting sport events: 10 for men and seven for women. Shooters compete in four different categories: five events with rifles, one event with a moving target, five more with pistols, and six events with shotguns.

Did You Know?

Archery was first introduced to the modern day Olympic games in 1900.

Giving Back to Nature

Conservation is the protection, preservation, management, or restoration of wildlife and of natural resources like forests, soil, and water. It is mostly handled by state conservation departments. They get nearly all of their funding from hunting licenses and special taxes on hunting equipment.

In most states, there is no other tax or funding base for these programs. The ratio of funding from licenses and taxes on hunting equipment varies from state to state, but it still nearly all comes from hunters. No federal money is used in statewide conservation.

Every year, hunters contribute hundreds of millions of dollars for conservation programs that benefit many wildlife species.

The Federal Duck Stamp

The U.S. Congress passed the Migratory Bird Hunting Stamp Act in 1934. This requires waterfowl hunters to buy the Federal Duck Stamp. Proceeds from this stamp have bought nearly 5 million acres (2 million hectares) of habitat for waterfowl and other wildlife species.

Where the Buffalo Roam

In the United States, what you hunt depends largely on where you live and what animals you're allowed to hunt there. A look around the vast country will show a wide range of birds, water fowl, and small and large game.

Utah: mountain lion, cougar, Shiraz moose

Colorado: moose, buffalo, bighorn sheep

Texas: quail, coyote, bobcat

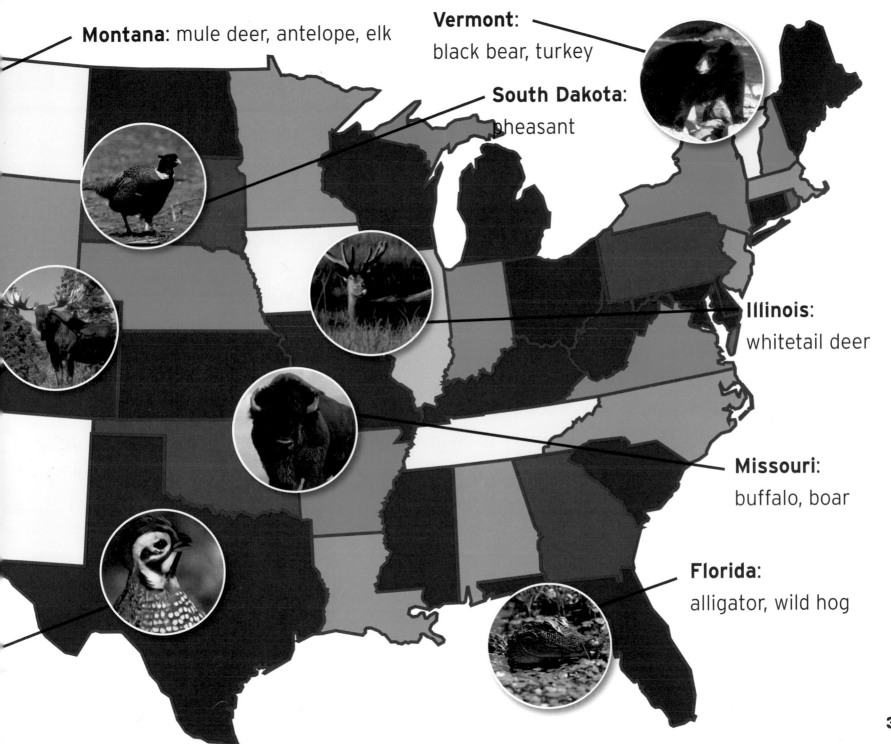

Montana: mule deer, antelope, elk

Vermont: black bear, turkey

South Dakota: pheasant

Illinois: whitetail deer

Missouri: buffalo, boar

Florida: alligator, wild hog

Global Game

Hunting is popular all around the world. The basic principles of hunting are the same from country to country, but often the type of game is very different.

The British were famous for their foxhunts. Although it was banned in 2005, for centuries the foxhunt was a very popular social outing for the upper class and even the royal family.

Pheasant hunting is common in many parts of the United States, Europe, and Asia. This is because there is an abundance of pheasants in these locations, and pheasant is considered very good to eat. A quick search through any cookbook will reveal many pheasant recipes.

Hunters who prefer to hunt big game, such as elephants and zebras, may go on safari in Africa. Big game hunting is also popular in New Zealand, where hunters seek out red stags, wallabies, and rams. Hunting big game can be dangerous and expensive. Big game outings require a lot of planning and organization, and should only be attempted by the most experienced of hunters.

Plains zebras drink water in Tanzania, Africa.

Teddy and Ted's Excellent Adventures

THEODORE ROOSEVELT

U.S. President Theodore "Teddy" Roosevelt was an avid hunter. He was especially fond of big game hunting and wrote a number of essays and books, including *The Wilderness Hunter*. Like most ethical hunters, Roosevelt was passionate about the conservation of natural lands and resources. During his time in office, he declared millions of acres of U.S. land as protected national forests, bird reservations, and game preserves, including the Grand Canyon, Mesa Verde, and Glacier national parks.

TED NUGENT

Rock 'n' roll legend Ted Nugent is well known for his passion and devotion to hunting. Nugent came from a long family line of hunters and began hunting before he even picked up a guitar! He owns his own supply store and even sells his own beef jerky. Nugent's greatest contribution to young hunters is his Kamp for Kids, where kids and teens from 9 to 15 years of age are taught about hunting, safety, wildlife, conservation, and the importance of having respect for nature and all its creatures.

What Happened When?

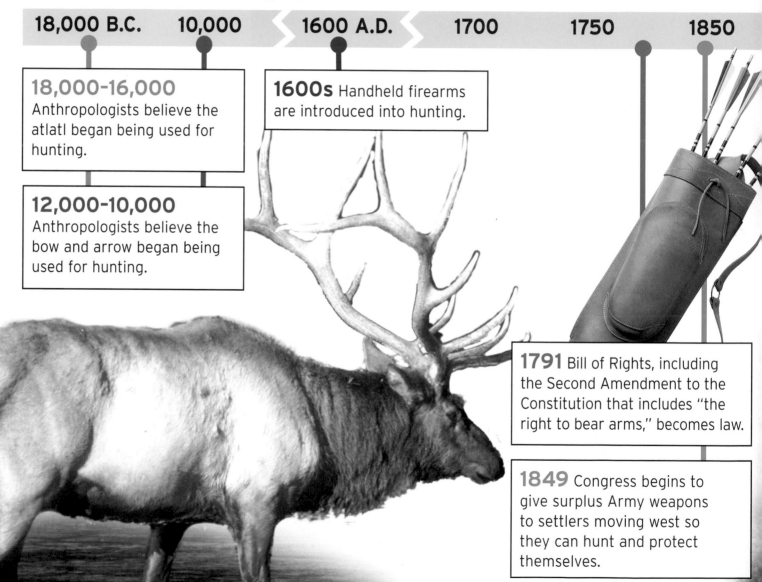

| 18,000 B.C. | 10,000 | 1600 A.D. | 1700 | 1750 | 1850 |

18,000–16,000 Anthropologists believe the atlatl began being used for hunting.

12,000–10,000 Anthropologists believe the bow and arrow began being used for hunting.

1600s Handheld firearms are introduced into hunting.

1791 Bill of Rights, including the Second Amendment to the Constitution that includes "the right to bear arms," becomes law.

1849 Congress begins to give surplus Army weapons to settlers moving west so they can hunt and protect themselves.

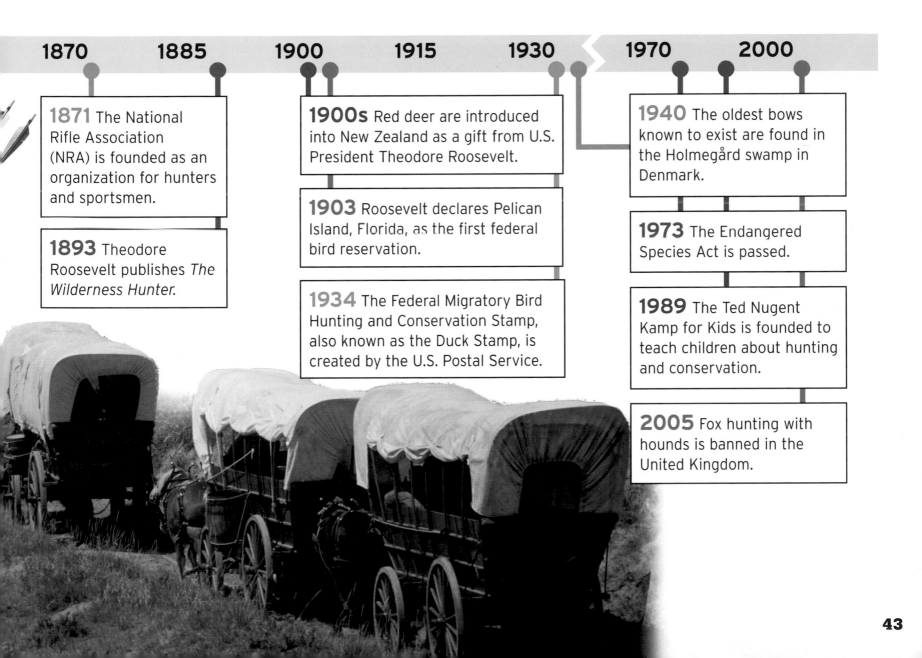

1870   **1885**   **1900**   **1915**   **1930**   **1970**   **2000**

1871 The National Rifle Association (NRA) is founded as an organization for hunters and sportsmen.

1893 Theodore Roosevelt publishes *The Wilderness Hunter.*

1900s Red deer are introduced into New Zealand as a gift from U.S. President Theodore Roosevelt.

1903 Roosevelt declares Pelican Island, Florida, as the first federal bird reservation.

1934 The Federal Migratory Bird Hunting and Conservation Stamp, also known as the Duck Stamp, is created by the U.S. Postal Service.

1940 The oldest bows known to exist are found in the Holmegård swamp in Denmark.

1973 The Endangered Species Act is passed.

1989 The Ted Nugent Kamp for Kids is founded to teach children about hunting and conservation.

2005 Fox hunting with hounds is banned in the United Kingdom.

Fun Hunting Facts

Hunting directions written in Medieval Europe have been found that describe how to hunt unicorns! This is pretty amazing, considering that there's no proof unicorns ever existed.

Prehistoric humans invented jerky (dried meats) as a way of preserving meats since there was no refrigeration.

In Alaska black bears are not just black. Some can have blue or even white fur.

New York City

An estimated 20 million to 25 million whitetail deer live in North America. That's about three times the population of New York City!

Many animal hides, including moose, elk, and deer, are used to make drums and other percussion instruments.

Cougars are a deer's worst enemy. Cougars kill more deer than hunters do.

Ted Nugent began bowhunting three years before learning how to play a guitar. He has more experience hunting than he does playing music!

Hunting Words to Know

ammunition: projectiles like bullets and shot, that can be fired from guns or propelled in some way

archery: the art, sport, or skill of shooting with a bow and arrow

BB: a standard size of lead pellet that measures $7/40$ of an inch (0.44 cm) in diameter; used in air rifles

bird dog: a dog used to hunt game birds

bird shot: small lead shot for shotgun shells

blind: a shelter for concealing hunters or nature photographers

bow and arrow: a weapon consisting of arrows and the bow to shoot them

buck: the adult male of some animals, such as the deer, antelope, or rabbit

camouflage: anything that conceals a person or equipment by making them appear to be part of the natural surroundings

ecosystem: an ecological community together with its environment, functioning as a unit

field dressing: preparing a recently killed animal in order to bring down the body temperature; this process keeps the meat fresh and usable

firearm: a weapon, especially a pistol or rifle, capable of firing a projectile (ammunition) and using an explosive charge to propel it

fowl: any bird, such as the duck, goose, turkey, or pheasant, that is used as food or hunted as game

game: wild animals, birds, or fish hunted for food or sport

habitat: the area or environment where an animal lives

hide: the skin of an animal, especially the thick tough skin or pelt of a large animal

pellet: a bullet or piece of small shot

poaching: to take fish or game in a forbidden area or fish or game that is against the law to take

prey: an animal hunted or caught for food

rifle: type of firearm with a long barrel

scope: an instrument for viewing or observing; usually a magnified view

season: a period each year at the same time, characterized by certain events, festivities, or crops

shotgun: a firearm similar to a rifle, except it shoots shot (more than one pellet) instead of a single bullet

sights: the part of a weapon that is used for aiming by alignment

telescope: an object that allows observation of distant objects

tracking: to follow the tracks of

tree stand: equipment that allows a person to sit up in a tree; used by hunters to avoid being detected by animals

GLOSSARY
Other Words to Know

ancestors: member of a person's family who lived a long time ago

avid: showing a great deal of interest or enthusiasm

coexist: to exist together at the same time or in the same place

essential: very important, necessary

ethical: having to do with right and wrong behavior

etiquette: set of rules about socially acceptable behavior

extinction: the process of becoming extinct; no longer existing

overpopulation: too much population in an area to the point of overcrowding, the overuse of natural resources, or environmental damage

seminar: a meeting to exchange ideas or learn about a topic

technology: the use of science and engineering to accomplish practical things

Where To Learn More

AT THE LIBRARY

Sorrells, Brian J. *Beginner's Guide to Traditional Archery*. Mechanicsburg, Penn.: Stackpole Books, 2004.

Phillips, John. *Secrets to Successful Turkey Hunting (Outdoor Classics Field Guide)*. Chaska, Minn.: Publishing Solutions, 2004.

ON THE ROAD

Ted Nugent Kamp for Kids
6420 Cowell
Brighton, Mich. 48116
888/777-6958
www.tnkfk.com

ON THE WEB

For more information on HUNTING, use FactHound to track down Web sites related to this book.

1. Go to www.facthound.com
2. Type in this book ID: 0756516803
3. Click on the *Fetch It* button.

Your trusty FactHound will fetch the best Web sites for you!

INDEX

ABOUT THE AUTHOR

Jef Wilson grew up in Missouri where he enjoyed many outdoor nature activities, including hiking, camping, and hunting. Throughout North America, he has explored a variety of trails and landscapes by foot or by bicycle. He is currently a writer and illustrator in educational publishing. He lives in New Jersey where he continues to enjoy and explore the great outdoors with his two young sons, Arlo and Cage.